FROM NOVICE TO NETWORK MARKETING PRO

Understanding Network Marketing

Emmanuel Olamide

Copyright © 2024 Emmanuel Olamide

All rights reserved

ISBN: 9798328847490

To all the dreamers and doers,

This book is dedicated to those who dare to step into the world of network marketing with ambition, determination, and an unwavering belief in their potential. To the novices who are just beginning their journey and to the seasoned professionals who continue to push the boundaries of success.

To my family and friends, whose support and encouragement have been the bedrock of my endeavors. Your love and belief in me have fueled my passion and perseverance.

To my mentors "Mr Moses Ozil" and peers in the network marketing industry, who have *generously shared their wisdom and experiences, inspiring me to grow and excel.*

And to every individual striving to transform their lives and achieve their dreams through network marketing, may this book serve as a guide, a resource, and a source of inspiration. Your dedication, resilience, and continuous pursuit of excellence are the true essence of success.

Thank you for embarking on this journey with me. Together, we will turn aspirations into achievements and build a legacy of lasting success.

With gratitude and respect,

Emmanuel Olamide

CONTENTS

Part 1: Section 1 - Introduction to Network Marketing

Part 1: Section 2 - The Network Marketing Industry

Part 1: Section 3 - Myths and Realities of Network Marketing

Acknowledgement

About The Author

From Novice to Network Marketing Pro

PART 1: SECTION 1 - INTRODUCTION TO NETWORK MARKETING

Welcome to "Understanding Network Marketing," the first installment in our "From Novice to Network Marketing Pro" series. This ebook is your gateway to comprehending the fundamentals of network marketing, an industry that offers vast opportunities for those willing to learn and grow. Whether you're a complete novice or someone looking to solidify your foundational knowledge, this ebook will equip you with the essential insights needed to embark on a successful network marketing journey.

Definition and Overview

Network marketing, also known as multilevel marketing (MLM), is a business model that relies on person-to-person sales by independent representatives, often working from home. Unlike traditional sales models, network marketing leverages your personal network to grow your business and generate income.

At its core, network marketing involves the promotion and sale of products or services through a network of distributors. These distributors are incentivized not only to sell products directly to consumers but also to recruit new distributors into their network. This creates multiple levels of sales representatives, hence the term multilevel marketing.

The unique appeal of network marketing lies in its simplicity and potential for exponential growth. With relatively low startup costs and minimal overhead, it provides an accessible pathway for aspiring entrepreneurs to start their own business. By harnessing the power of personal relationships and word-of-mouth marketing, network marketing allows individuals to build a business on their terms, often with flexible working hours and the ability to work from anywhere.

History and Evolution

The history of network marketing dates back to the early 20th century, with the concept gaining traction as a viable business model in the 1940s and 1950s. One of the earliest and most influential companies in this space was Nutrilite, a dietary supplement company that utilized a direct selling approach. Nutrilite's success laid the groundwork for the network marketing industry, demonstrating the potential of this unique business model.

In the 1950s, Amway (short for "American Way") emerged as a pioneer in the network marketing industry. Amway's founders, Rich DeVos and Jay Van Andel, introduced a compensation plan that rewarded distributors not only for their sales but also for the sales made by the distributors they recruited. This innovation marked a significant shift in the industry, setting the stage for the multilevel compensation structures that define network marketing today.

The 1960s and 1970s saw the rise of other notable companies, such as Mary Kay and Tupperware, which further popularized the network marketing model. These companies leveraged home parties and social gatherings as a means of product demonstration and sales, emphasizing the importance of personal relationships in driving business growth.

In recent decades, network marketing has continued to evolve, adapting to changing consumer behaviors and technological advancements. The rise of the internet and social media has transformed how distributors connect with potential customers and recruits, enabling them to reach a broader audience and expand their networks more efficiently. Today, network marketing is a global industry with billions of dollars in annual sales and millions of participants worldwide.

Key Concepts and Terminology

To navigate the world of network marketing effectively, it's crucial to understand its key concepts and terminology. Here are a few essential terms you will encounter:

- **Upline and Downline**: Your upline consists of the people who recruited you into the business, while your downline includes the individuals you recruit. Your success is interconnected, as you earn commissions not only from your sales but also from the sales made by your downline.
- **Compensation Plan**: This is the structure that outlines how you will be paid. It includes details on commissions, bonuses, and other incentives. Understanding your company's compensation plan is vital for maximizing your earnings.
- **Residual Income**: One of the most appealing aspects of network marketing is the potential for residual income. This means you can continue to earn money from your efforts long after the initial sale, providing a steady income stream.

- **Recruitment**: The process of bringing new individuals into your network marketing business. Effective recruitment strategies are essential for expanding your network and increasing your earning potential.
- **Duplication**: A key principle in network marketing, duplication involves teaching your downline to replicate your successful strategies and methods. By creating a system that can be easily duplicated, you can ensure consistent growth and success within your network.
- **Leadership and Training**: As you build your network, developing leadership skills and providing ongoing training to your downline becomes crucial. Strong leaders inspire and motivate their teams, driving collective success.

By understanding these key concepts and the terminology used in network marketing, you'll be better equipped to navigate the industry and make informed decisions that contribute to your success.

"Introduction to Network Marketing" sets the stage for your journey into the dynamic world of network marketing. By grasping the definition, history, and key concepts of this industry, you'll lay a strong foundation for your business. As you progress through this ebook and the subsequent volumes in the series, you'll gain valuable insights and practical knowledge that will empower you to take confident steps toward your goals. Welcome to the exciting world of network marketing—your journey begins here!

PART 1: SECTION 2 - THE NETWORK MARKETING INDUSTRY

Welcome to the second section of "Understanding Network Marketing." In this section, we delve into the current landscape of the network marketing industry. We will explore its market size and growth, identify major players and companies, and examine current trends and future predictions. By understanding these aspects, you'll gain a comprehensive view of the industry and its potential for your business journey.

Market Size and Growth

The network marketing industry has experienced significant growth over the past few decades, establishing itself as a major player in the global economy. As of recent estimates, the industry generates over $180 billion in annual sales worldwide, involving millions of independent distributors in hundreds of countries.

This impressive market size is driven by several factors:

1. **Low Entry Barriers**: Network marketing offers a low-cost entry point for aspiring entrepreneurs, allowing individuals from various backgrounds to start their own business without substantial capital investment.
2. **Global Reach**: With advancements in technology and communication, network marketing has transcended geographical boundaries, enabling distributors to reach a global audience and expand their networks internationally.
3. **Consumer Trust**: Products sold through network marketing are often recommended by trusted friends and family members, fostering a high level of consumer trust and loyalty.
4. **Flexible Business Model**: The flexibility of network marketing, allowing distributors to work part-time or full-time, appeals to a wide range of individuals, from stay-at-home parents to full-time

professionals seeking additional income streams.

Major Players and Companies

Several companies have become synonymous with network marketing, thanks to their longevity, innovation, and significant market impact. Here are some of the major players in the industry:

1. **Amway**: Founded in 1959, Amway is one of the pioneers of network marketing. It offers a wide range of products, including health, beauty, and home care items. Amway's global reach and robust compensation plan have made it a leader in the industry.
2. **Herbalife**: Specializing in nutrition, weight management, and personal care products, Herbalife has been a major force in network marketing since its inception in 1980. The company's focus on health and wellness has resonated with consumers worldwide.
3. **Avon**: Known for its beauty and skincare products, Avon has a long history dating back to 1886. While it operates as a direct selling company, it incorporates many network

marketing principles, particularly in its compensation structure.
4. **Mary Kay**: Founded in 1963, Mary Kay has become a household name in the beauty industry. Its strong emphasis on empowering women through entrepreneurship has contributed to its widespread success.
5. **Nu Skin**: This company offers anti-aging products and nutritional supplements. Founded in 1984, Nu Skin has gained a reputation for innovation and high-quality products, attracting a large network of distributors.
6. **Tupperware**: Famous for its innovative food storage solutions, Tupperware has been a key player in direct selling since the 1940s. Its party-based selling approach has become a model for many network marketing companies.

Current Trends and Future Predictions

The network marketing industry is continuously evolving, influenced by technological advancements, changing consumer preferences, and economic shifts. Here are some current trends and future predictions shaping the industry:

1. **Digital Transformation**: The rise of social media and digital platforms has revolutionized network marketing. Distributors are increasingly leveraging these tools to connect with customers, host virtual events, and manage their businesses online. This trend is expected to continue, with more companies investing in digital infrastructure and training.
2. **Health and Wellness Focus**: Consumer interest in health and wellness products has surged, driven by a growing awareness of healthy living and preventative care. Network marketing companies specializing in nutritional supplements, fitness products, and wellness programs are likely to see continued growth.
3. **Personal Branding**: As competition within the industry intensifies, distributors are focusing on personal branding to differentiate themselves. Building a strong personal brand helps distributors establish credibility, attract a loyal customer base, and recruit effectively.
4. **Sustainable and Ethical Practices**: Consumers are increasingly demanding transparency,

sustainability, and ethical practices from businesses. Network marketing companies that prioritize eco-friendly products, ethical sourcing, and social responsibility are gaining a competitive edge.

5. **Gen Z and Millennial Engagement**: Younger generations, particularly Millennials and Gen Z, are showing interest in network marketing as a flexible and entrepreneurial career option. Companies are adapting their strategies to appeal to these tech-savvy and socially conscious individuals.

6. **Global Expansion**: As emerging markets continue to grow, network marketing companies are expanding their operations into new regions. This global expansion presents opportunities for distributors to tap into new customer bases and diversify their networks.

7. **Regulatory Scrutiny**: With the increasing popularity of network marketing, regulatory bodies are paying closer attention to the industry. Companies are expected to adhere to stricter compliance standards, ensuring transparency and protecting distributors and consumers alike.

The network marketing industry offers a dynamic and evolving landscape filled with opportunities for growth and success. By understanding the market size and growth, recognizing the major players and companies, and staying abreast of current trends and future predictions, you can navigate this industry more effectively and make informed decisions for your business. As you continue your journey through this ebook, you'll gain further insights and practical knowledge to build a thriving network marketing career. Welcome to the exciting world of network marketing—your journey continues here!

PART 1: SECTION 3 - MYTHS AND REALITIES OF NETWORK MARKETING

Welcome to the third section of "Understanding Network Marketing." In this section, we will address some of the most common misconceptions about network marketing, discuss important legal and ethical considerations, and compare success stories with failures to provide a balanced perspective on the industry. By dispelling myths and understanding the realities, you will be better prepared to navigate the challenges and seize the opportunities that network marketing offers.

Common Misconceptions

Network marketing is often misunderstood, leading to a range of misconceptions that can deter potential entrepreneurs. Here are some of the most prevalent myths and the truths behind them:

1. **"Network marketing is a pyramid scheme."**
   - **Reality**: While network marketing and pyramid schemes might appear similar on the surface, they are fundamentally different. Pyramid schemes are illegal and unsustainable because they rely on recruiting new members without offering a legitimate product or service. In contrast, network marketing involves the sale of real products or services, and distributors earn commissions based on sales, not just recruitment.
2. **"You need to be a natural salesperson to succeed."**
   - **Reality**: Success in network marketing is not limited to those with sales experience. While effective communication and interpersonal skills are valuable, the industry offers extensive training and support to help individuals develop these abilities. Success is often driven by

dedication, persistence, and the ability to build and maintain relationships.

3. **"Only the people at the top make money."**
   - **Reality**: Earnings in network marketing are based on individual effort and the ability to build a successful team. While those who join early and work hard may have an advantage, newcomers can also achieve significant success through consistent effort and strategic planning. The compensation plans in legitimate network marketing companies are designed to reward performance at all levels.

4. **"It's a get-rich-quick scheme."**
   - **Reality**: Network marketing requires hard work, time, and persistence. While it offers the potential for significant income, success is typically the result of sustained effort and the ability to build and support a team. Promises of quick and easy riches are misleading and should be viewed with skepticism.

5. **"Products are overpriced and of low quality."**
   - **Reality**: Many network marketing companies offer high-quality products that are competitively

priced. The perception of overpriced products often stems from the additional value provided by personal consultation and support from distributors. Successful companies focus on delivering genuine value to their customers.

Legal and Ethical Considerations

Operating within the legal and ethical boundaries is crucial for the success and sustainability of any network marketing business. Here are some important considerations:

1. **Compliance with Regulations**: Network marketing companies must comply with federal, state, and international laws governing business operations and direct selling. This includes adhering to consumer protection laws, truthful advertising, and transparent compensation plans.
2. **Avoiding Pyramid Schemes**: It's essential to distinguish legitimate network marketing from pyramid schemes. Legitimate companies emphasize product sales and offer

tangible value. Be wary of any opportunity that prioritizes recruitment over product sales or requires significant upfront investments without providing real products.

3. **Transparent Income Claims**: Ethical network marketing companies provide realistic and transparent information about income potential. Avoid making exaggerated income claims or guaranteeing specific earnings, as this can be misleading and legally problematic.
4. **Ethical Recruiting Practices**: Recruiting new distributors should be based on honesty and transparency. Ensure that potential recruits fully understand the business model, compensation plan, and the effort required to succeed.
5. **Consumer Protection**: Protecting consumers' interests is paramount. This includes offering fair return policies, providing accurate product information, and ensuring customer satisfaction.

Success Stories vs. Failures

Network marketing has produced both remarkable success stories and notable failures. Understanding the factors behind these outcomes can provide valuable insights:

1. **Success Stories:**
   - **Example 1: Mary Kay Ash**: The founder of Mary Kay Cosmetics started her business with a small investment and a vision to empower women. Through perseverance, innovative strategies, and a strong focus on personal development, she built a global beauty empire.
   - **Example 2: Rich DeVos and Jay Van Andel**: The founders of Amway turned their entrepreneurial spirit and belief in the direct selling model into one of the largest and most successful network marketing companies in the world.
2. Common factors in these success stories include a clear vision, innovative strategies, strong leadership, and a commitment to training and supporting their distributors.
3. **Failures:**
   - **Example 1: BurnLounge**: This company was shut down by the Federal Trade Commission (FTC) for operating as a pyramid scheme.

It focused more on recruiting new members than selling products, leading to its downfall.
    - **Example 2: Fortune Hi-Tech Marketing**: Another company that faced legal action for deceptive practices and operating as a pyramid scheme. The lack of legitimate product sales and emphasis on recruitment led to its closure.
4. Common factors in these failures include an overemphasis on recruitment, lack of a legitimate product or service, misleading income claims, and failure to comply with legal standards.

"Myths and Realities of Network Marketing" aims to provide a balanced perspective on the network marketing industry. By dispelling common misconceptions, understanding legal and ethical considerations, and learning from both success stories and failures, you can approach your network marketing business with a well-informed and realistic mindset. As you continue to explore the industry through this ebook, you'll be better equipped to navigate challenges and leverage opportunities for your success. Welcome to the world of network marketing—your journey continues here!

ACKNOWLEDGEMENT

First and foremost, I would like to express my deepest gratitude to my family. Your unwavering support, encouragement, and love have been the cornerstone of my journey. To my parents, for instilling in me the values of hard work and perseverance, and to my spouse and children, for being my greatest cheerleaders and a constant source of inspiration.

A heartfelt thank you to my mentors and peers in the network marketing industry. Your guidance, wisdom, and shared experiences have been invaluable in shaping my career. Your contributions to my growth and success are immeasurable.

To my friends and colleagues who believed in me and supported my vision, your encouragement and faith have driven me to push boundaries and strive for excellence. Thank you for being there every step of the way.

I am deeply grateful to the network marketing community, whose collective knowledge and experiences have enriched my understanding of the industry. Your dedication and passion continue to inspire me every day.

Special thanks to my editor and publishing team for their expertise, patience, and hard work in bringing this book to life. Your efforts have been instrumental in ensuring that this work reaches its full potential.

Lastly, to all the readers and aspiring network marketers, this book is for you. Your ambition and determination to achieve greatness inspire me. I hope that this book serves as a valuable resource on your journey to success.

Thank you all for being part of this incredible journey. Your support and belief in me have made this possible.

With profound gratitude,

Emmanuel Olamide

ABOUT THE AUTHOR

Emmanuel Olamide

Emmanuel Olamide is a distinguished network marketing professional with over a decade of experience in the industry. His journey from a novice to a highly successful network marketing pro is a testament to his unwavering dedication, innovative strategies, and exceptional leadership skills. Emmanuel's expertise spans across various facets of network marketing, including team building, digital marketing, and strategic planning.

Driven by a passion for empowering others, Emmanuel has dedicated his career to helping aspiring network marketers unlock their potential and achieve their dreams. He has mentored countless individuals, guiding them through the complexities of the industry and equipping them with the tools and knowledge needed for success.

Emmanuel is known for his practical insights, motivational approach, and commitment to continuous learning. His ability to adapt to changing market dynamics and leverage new technologies has positioned him as a thought leader in the network marketing community.

In addition to his professional accomplishments, Emmanuel is a sought-after speaker and trainer, regularly sharing his expertise at industry conferences and events. His engaging style and deep understanding of the network marketing landscape make his presentations both informative and inspiring.

"From Novice to Network Marketing Pro" is a culmination of Emmanuel's extensive experience and insights. Through this series, he aims to provide a comprehensive guide for individuals at all stages of their network marketing journey, offering actionable strategies and invaluable wisdom.

Emmanuel Olamide resides in Nigeria, where he continues to inspire and lead by example, demonstrating that with the right mindset and dedication, anyone can achieve extraordinary success in network marketing.

FROM NOVICE TO NETWORK MARKETING PRO

Are you ready to transform your network marketing dreams into reality? Dive into the comprehensive ebook series "From Novice to Network Marketing Pro" and embark on a journey from the basics to the pinnacle of success in the network marketing world. This series is designed for aspiring network marketers, seasoned professionals seeking to refine their skills, and anyone curious about the potential of this dynamic industry.

Volume 1: Understanding Network Marketing
Unlock the foundational knowledge necessary for a successful network marketing career. Learn about the industry's history, key concepts, and common myths. Gain insight into market trends and discover the realities behind the network marketing business model.

Volume 2: Getting Started
Find out how to choose the right network

marketing company that aligns with your values and goals. This volume covers everything from setting up your business, establishing clear objectives, and creating a robust business plan to building a personal brand that stands out in a crowded marketplace.

Volume 3: Building Your Network
Master the art of prospecting and lead generation, and learn effective communication and follow-up techniques. This volume provides strategies for hosting impactful events and presentations, both in-person and online, to grow and maintain a thriving network.

Volume 4: Growing and Scaling Your Business
Develop your leadership skills and learn how to build, motivate, and retain a strong team. Discover advanced marketing strategies, including digital marketing, content creation, and email campaigns, to expand your reach and scale your business efficiently.

Volume 5: Achieving Long-Term Success
Learn how to monitor and measure your performance using key metrics, overcome common challenges, and sustain growth over the long term. This volume guides you through exploring new markets, diversifying income streams, and planning for a prosperous future.

"From Novice to Network Marketing Pro" is

more than just a series of ebooks—it's a complete guide to achieving success in the network marketing industry. With practical advice, proven strategies, and motivational insights, this series will equip you with the tools you need to rise from a beginner to a network marketing expert. Whether you're just starting out or looking to enhance your skills, this series is your essential companion on the road to network marketing success.

Understanding Network Marketing

Getting Started

Building Your Network

Growing and Scaling Your Business

Achieving Long-Term Success

www.ingramcontent.com/pod-product-compliance
Lightning Source LLC
Chambersburg PA
CBHW072057230526
45479CB00010B/1118